Wake Up:
The Power of Good Morning

A Story of Growth, Transformation, and Awakenings

Antonella Agostini

BALBOA
PRESS
A DIVISION OF HAY HOUSE

a.a.

Balboa Press books may be ordered through booksellers or by contacting:

Balboa Press
A Division of Hay House
1663 Liberty Drive
Bloomington, IN 47403
www.balboapress.com.au
1 (877) 407-4847

Print information available on the last page.

ISBN: 978-1-9822-3368-6 (sc)
ISBN: 978-1-9822-3370-9 (hc)
ISBN: 978-1-9822-3369-3 (e)

Library of Congress Control Number: 2019913183

Balboa Press rev. date: 11/04/2019

a.a.

Dedication

To my friends, El and James.

Without you, my good mornings would never have been born.

Thank you for seeing me as I truly am. I love you both.

And to the loves of my life,

Olivia and Joe

Jericho and Hazel

No words can express the love I feel for all of you.

a.a.

Acknowledgement

Thank you to Balboa Press, and all its members for staying with me through the process of publishing my very first book. It's been an awesome journey as we tweak this raw project to a standard of excellence.

Thank you to my Facebook family for always being a light that I can find in moments of darkness. Iam inspired by your tenacity to seek all that is good in the world.

Thank you to God for being a constant in my life. I know that I am loved and cherished.

Thank you to the Universe. The Universe is my companion. I am in the flow of its eternal love, wisdom, peace and joy. Thank you for all of the surprises you have given me.

Thank you to all the men that have loved me and hurt me. My journey does not exist without you.

And finally, thank you to the love of my life. I know you exist, I just don't know where yet. I do this all for you.

a.a.

Contents

Dedication vii

Acknowledgement...ix

Preface xiii

iSPEEK xix

Chapter 1   Positivity..1

Chapter 2   Inspiration 13

Chapter 3   Spirituality...21

Chapter 4   Empowerment 39

Chapter 5   Encouragement..61

Chapter 6   K-Creativity..75

Chapter 7   Evolution 89

About the Reading List 93

Reading List and Online Meditations 95

a.a.

Preface

This book reveals a blueprint for awakening the soul. These discoveries have been made through my healing process and real-life experiences.

It all started in 2011.

I attended a one-day seminar that covered topics such as the law of attraction and relationships. It was a very intimate session led by a teacher whom I had met through a series of adult learning classes. She was a warm, loving, and a good-hearted person who completely mesmerized me. At that time in my life, she was instrumental in encouraging me, nurturing me, and showing me unconditional love. Subsequently, she became a very good friend of mine.

During a seminar, the topic of finding the love of my life creeped into the discussion. My teacher asked, "What is one of the qualities about being in a relationship that you love so much?" The first thing that I thought about was getting a good-morning message from my love. It would be a text or message that assured me that I was loved and cared for. With her radiating smile, she looked at me and said, "Well, if you want a good morning, then give a good morning."

There was a spark, and a fire had been lit within me. A newfound hope and enthusiasm arose with the belief that this might lead to the healthy and loving relationship I wanted so badly. I gathered phone numbers and email addresses, and I began my pursuit of happily ever after with every morning I woke up.

Over the past few years, as I continued with the good-morning messages, their hidden power has evolved into a stepping-stone that has changed me and given me a new foundation that guides and directs the way I live my life.

I could see that there was a pattern forming as I traveled my path of self-discovery and completely immersed myself in solving the puzzle that was my life. This was all fueled by my deep-down desire to be in love. The pattern illuminated a formula I followed that could eventually lead to my dream relationship.

The power of the good mornings initiated all of it, unveiling more of my true spirit, and it has become the signature of my soul.

As I continue to grow and evolve, so does the formula. I am uncovering more than I ever expected. I woke up. I revealed that I can design my reality through a blueprint that is drawn by the guidelines of who I am. I am creating my dreams and wishes, and I am building them into reality.

The components of the formula are inspired by my story—the story of a girl who is compelled to be in love.

iSPEEK

a.a.

As I created the good-morning messages, I began using hashtags for specific social media platforms. Inspiration struck! There were six words that stood out more than others, and I continued seeing the repetition of these words. As I meditated on these words more and more, one day, the acronym popped into my head: iSPEEK.

i-inspiration
S-spirituality
P-positivity
E-empowerment
E-encouragement
K-creativity

.

iSPEEK. It was time for me to speak.

I had to express my message, and at the same time, I had to make sure there was a pure intention behind the message. The vibration or frequency of these words—coupled with the pure intent in which they are used—allows any message to intensify. This results in strong emotions and feelings surfacing and the heart opening. It is a conscious effort about what I say and the way I say it. It is a philosophy that I practice, endorse, and share with the world.

iSPEEK. I speak with purpose.

It has taken much time to come out of my cocoon and share my experiences. The pursuit of a deep-down desire has grown a shy little girl and timid adolescent into a spiritual woman who is declaring inspiration, positivity, empowerment, encouragement, and divine creativity.

A purpose is born, and fulfillment showers my life.

Positivity

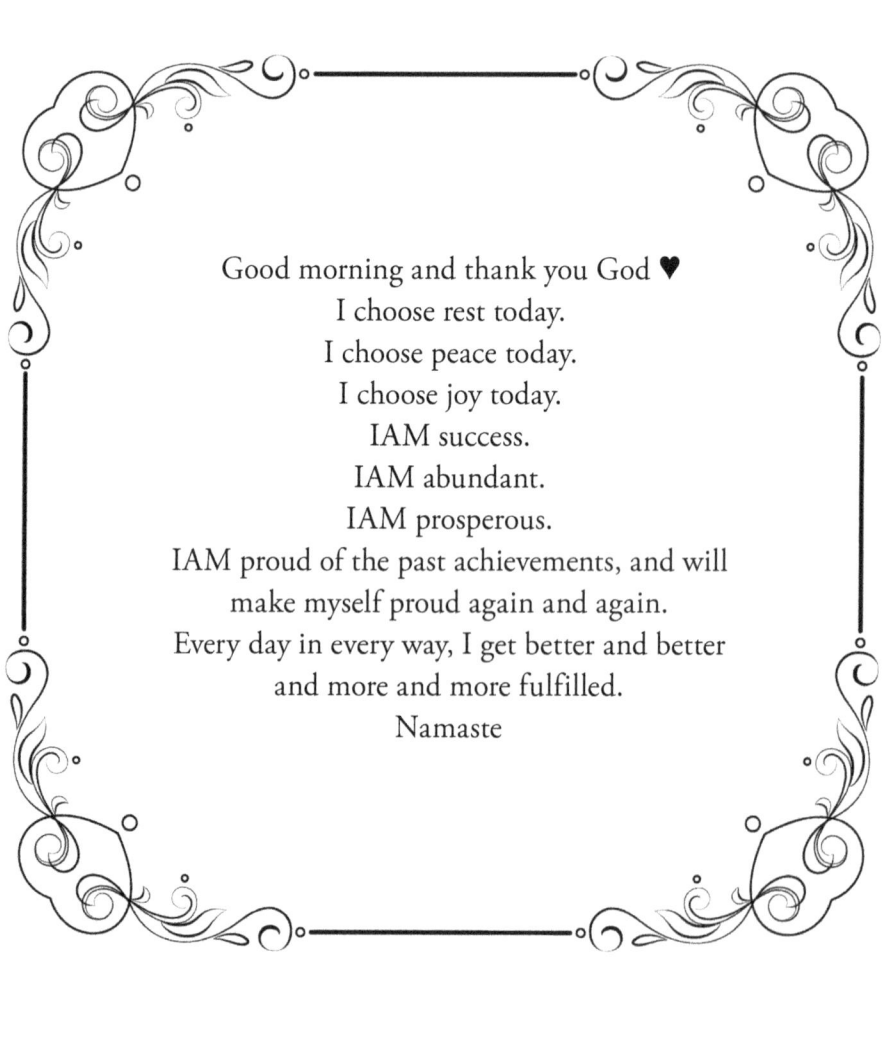

Good morning and thank you God ♥
I choose rest today.
I choose peace today.
I choose joy today.
IAM success.
IAM abundant.
IAM prosperous.
IAM proud of the past achievements, and will
make myself proud again and again.
Every day in every way, I get better and better
and more and more fulfilled.
Namaste

I was excited as I began my good-morning messages, and I dove into this fearlessly and passionately. My intention was propelled by the possibility that this would lead me closer to the love of my life.

I was extremely focused, and I was determined to make it work.

The most important quality of these good-morning messages had to be positivity. They had to convey some sort of feeling of enthusiasm and hope for the coming day.

This isn't difficult for me since I like to see the brighter side of life, and I am also intrinsically cheerful and joyful—most of the time!

In the past, however, I experienced a cataclysmic heartbreak. As I went through this time in my life, I succumbed to sadness and grief. I found myself at a level of emotion that was so low that there was a moment when I did not think I had the strength to move on.

As I moved through subsequent relationships, the heartbreaks and disillusionments continued. And with every heartbreak, I felt the possibility of slipping back into a deep coma of sorrow and heartache. I thought that if I failed in another relationship the weight of grief might sink me to the bottom of the ocean.

It took me a little while to build myself back up, and, thankfully, I did recover.

Along with the other tools and methods I discovered and talk about throughout this book, I knew that positivity would have to be at the forefront of my life if I did not want to succumb to discouragement, sadness, or grief.

Positivity begins with your thoughts.

You must keep your thoughts about yourself positive. In order to begin this process, you must start monitoring your thoughts. It may be beneficial to enlist some sort of counseling for this or seek out a person who knows you well enough and whom you trust to be honest with you. This can help you be objective with your self-analysis since you might not always recognize negative thought patterns or belief systems.

Your thoughts, feelings, and beliefs emit a frequency or vibrational energy into the Universe on a subconscious level. When you become aware that your subconscious plays a role in any harmful thought processes or belief systems, you can begin overriding it with new positive thoughts and beliefs.

This can be done, but it is necessary to first uncover or bring any adverse thoughts or beliefs to the surface to avoid additional self-trauma.

You must understand that the subconscious takes in any information and knowledge that it is given and stores it within you. That data directs the subconscious. This includes things you don't really believe and that do not resonate with the real you. The subconscious does not judge what it is fed. It only acquires the information and uses it to propel the behavior, choices, and actions that you will take.

Although you have a conscious awareness of what you want, you begin doing things or behaving in ways that are not congruent to what you say you want. This results in a conflict. You are saying one thing, but it's not manifesting for you, or an opposite result appears in your reality. You are repeatedly not getting what you want, and you may be confused and frustrated about why this is happening.

The first step in acquiring the answers to your inner conflicts

Good morning and thank you God ♥
I choose joy. ♥
I choose peace today. ♥
I choose silence. ♥
IAM positive. ♥
IAM worthy and IAM enough. ♥
IAM open to wealth and abundance. ♥
I love life and life loves me! ♥
I love you Universe. ♥
I love you God, and trust You. ♥
Namaste

is positivity. This is the first step, and it kick-starts the process of self-analysis. This can and will evolve as you look deeper within yourself.

When I send a good-morning message, it can reroute thoughts in a positive way. It is providing the reader with new information that is transferred to their subconscious as well as their conscious awareness. This is important because good thoughts will lead to feeling good or feeling better.

It may sound simple, but, eventually, the pendulum starts to acquire momentum in a different direction. This is where the awakening begins. At first, you may start to question your core beliefs, and this may come with some internal conflicts. It's hard to teach an old dog new tricks!

Yet this also positively enables you to change things for the better. You may begin behaving in ways that are foreign to you, but as the process becomes less threatening to your ego, it creates a new reality for you—a better reality.

Your new thoughts, which are much more congruent with your true being and your true desires, begin transforming you and giving you the life, you always wished for and that you deserve.

Positivity is connecting with your soul.

Your true nature is not your physical body. It is what some refer to as your *soul, higher self*, or *spirit*, and it is composed of intangibles that allow for immortality and infiniteness. Your true nature is composed of peace, joy, power, and—most of all—pure love.

It can be difficult for you to resonate with this kind of purity because the soul is also concealed by many unhappy or traumatic experiences. Some experiences may have been violent. These experiences could have happened in your current life, but they might also have accompanied you in prior lives.

There is an adverse effect when these experiences and the feelings

surrounding them sit within your soul for long periods. As negative experiences and memories continue to build up, your capacity to feel your soul diminishes, and you lose the ability to connect to your true essence. This does not mean that you lose your soul or that it can die. Your soul is immortal. Nothing can happen to it. It is about losing the opportunity to come into the soul's own awareness while in your physical body.

A weakened connection to your soul also creates a reality for you that resonates with emotions, such as guilt, shame, and the most negative, fear. Fear is the most negative emotion. These emotions contribute to negative thought patterns and belief systems, which is where negative thoughts are born. The emotion comes first, and then the thought follows. It begins a vicious cycle.

Because your emotions are so closely linked to connecting with your soul, it is imperative that you open your heart. Once your heart is moving toward expansiveness, it is the tie that begins opening an awareness to your true nature. As the heart opens, the soul can reawaken.

Awakening a wounded soul can be potent. However, with effort and courage, you can face these strong feelings and emotions and begin to heal. Healing will bring self-awareness of your true being. This leads to the capacity of living a physical existence on a soul level where one becomes enlightened. You possess understanding, compassion, peace, happiness, and an unconditional love for yourself and other living beings.

When I send a good-morning message that is positive, I believe it must move the reader's heart. It is an attempt to make a connection to the soul. In my experience, I have discovered a connection to the soul is best done through the heart. This is done by stirring and moving the heart so that it starts feeling positive emotions.

It is only with positive emotions that an existence with beautiful

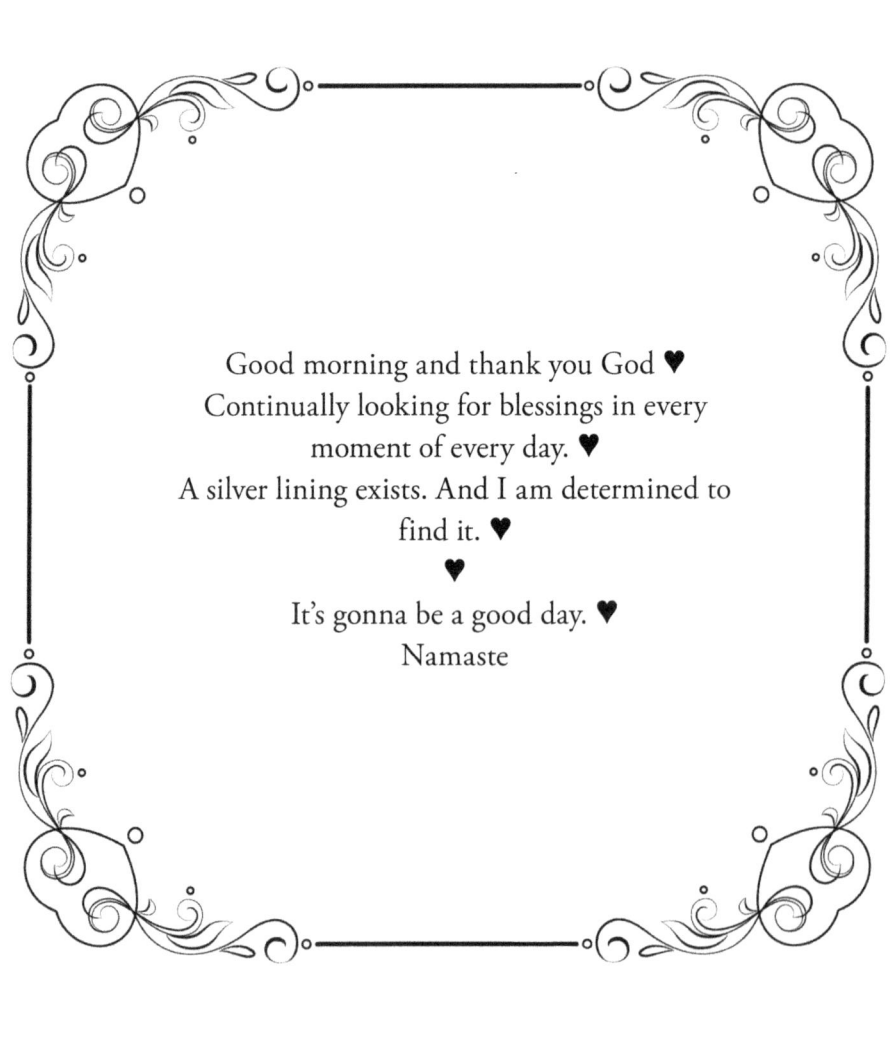

Good morning and thank you God ♥
Continually looking for blessings in every
moment of every day. ♥
A silver lining exists. And I am determined to
find it. ♥
♥
It's gonna be a good day. ♥
Namaste

and good experiences can begin. It commences a strong connection of who you really are.

Just as your negative experiences and memories can form a vicious cycle, positive emotions that lead to joyful experiences begin elevating you higher and higher.

Positivity is building your faith in God and the Universe.

There are moments when you might succumb to low feelings or energy; after all, you are human. However, in order to lift yourself out of these feelings, you can turn to the Universe and God. You can look for signs of their support and love for you. Start up a conversation with the Universe, God, or whomever you identify as your higher power. If you are paying attention, watching, and listening for their response, it does something powerful. It builds your faith. You begin knowing that there is an intangible being that is greater than you. You begin knowing there is more than what meets the eye. You know there is something working behind the scenes.

When I send a good-morning message—or any other message—it provides an opportunity for me to be a vessel through which the Universe and God use me to reach others with the positivity they may need in their lives.

2

Inspiration

Good morning and thank you God
I pray with you and for you.
May you be blessed, at peace, prosperous and
IN LOVE.
I wish you receive what you need as well as what
you want.

As I continued putting together my good-morning messages, monitoring my thoughts, connecting with my true essence, and building my faith, I encountered the beauty of inspiration.

I was inspired, and this continues in my life. I revere life more than I ever have. I learned that inspiration is more than just researching material. It is tapping into the divine within me. Inspiration is divinity itself. It is the source. It is the Universe. It is God.

Once I became open and receptive to inspiration, it became a chain reaction that linked truth to truth. I discovered that my thoughts were more and more pure. They were inspired from a universal consciousness. It is not a thought or belief that originates from an underlying memory, negative belief, or conditioning. It does not involve my ego, whether consciously or subconsciously.

I was inspired by many sources, authors, and books. I was stirred by engaging with friends and followers through social media and the material they posted on their platforms. It developed out of the practice of meditation, which has continually increased and evolved as I have grown.

Inspiration is synchronicity with the Universe.

When you begin to focus your attention on anything you desire, the Universe conspires to unfold all people, places, and things that are linked together to manifest that desire. The purer and more passionate the intent, the more clear, truthful, and divinely ordained the results. Once you are inspired, synchronicity takes motion. There are no coincidences.

It does take some effort to put faith in the unseen, but when you start shining the light of awareness on the signs and signals the Universe provides for you, it becomes apparent that everything happens for a reason. A plan is unfolding to manifest your deepest desires.

As I continued to research for my good-morning messages, I became more and more moved. I began noticing that one source of material would lead me to another that expressed the same truth. It was wonderful to see this unfold, and it strengthened my faith in the Universe. I was witnessing a common thread throughout the world and humanity.

Inspiration makes a connection with the heart and soul.

The source of inspiration is divine. The only way you can connect with it is by opening yourself through your heart and soul. This is where your divinity resides. You must feel in order to be inspired. Your deepest desires are created to trigger these feelings and emotions.

I was beginning to feel something happening as I created the good-morning messages. The more I saw the Universe in motion, the more my heart warmed—and it continues to do so. This happened more frequently as I paid more attention to the conversations the Universe was having with me.

I knew, underneath the scars of my heart, that something powerful was happening. I often participated in guided meditations that brought me to tears. I knew I was growing closer to my spirit. I started to feel that a powerful being lived beneath any pain, sadness, or anger I experienced. I knew it because it felt like home. It felt like something I knew but had never really experienced in this life. It was my soul.

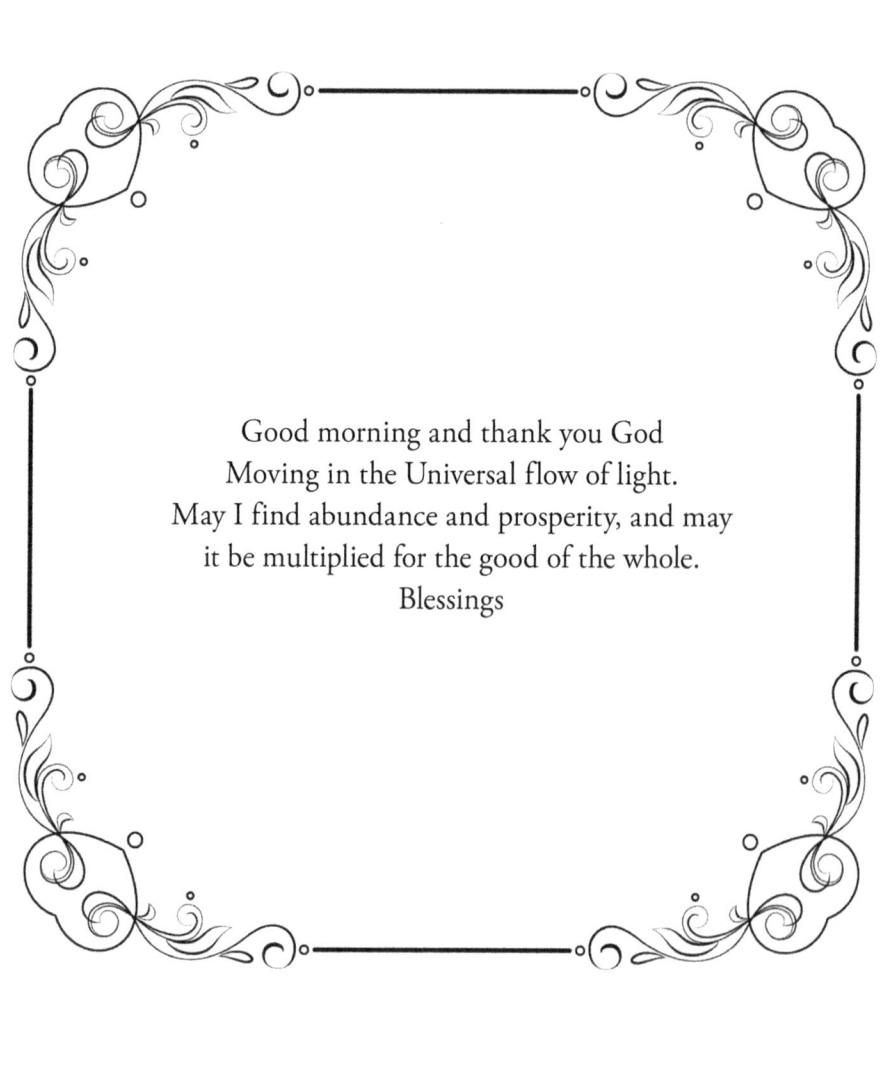

Good morning and thank you God
Moving in the Universal flow of light.
May I find abundance and prosperity, and may
it be multiplied for the good of the whole.
Blessings

Inspiration ripples into the Universe.

The best part of connecting to inspiration is inspiring others. There is an intrinsic quality to inspiration that compels you to express it and share it with the rest of your soul brothers and sisters around the world.

Soon you develop a desire to connect back to your spirit and allow any pain, sadness, or negativity to be peeled away.

The good-morning messages I began a few years ago have turned into the catalyst that I use as inspiration to lead me to open more hearts around the world. Knowing that even one heart has been moved gives me great joy. The awareness of my intention only makes this more powerful.

I accept that there is magic that ripples through the Universe with every attempt to inspire others, and I leave it to offer its benefit wherever it is needed.

I am grateful to my greatest and most significant desire of being in love if it helps open even one heart along the way.

I want to love everyone and everything. That is what I am inspired to do.

3

Spirituality

Good morning and thank you God ♥

IAM born again. ♥
I choose wisdom today. ♥
I choose life today. ♥
I choose love today. ♥
I choose FAITH. I know my life and Universe
get better and better, every day, in every way. ♥
What abundance awaits me? ♥
What love awaits me? ♥
What life awaits me? ♥
Namaste

My spirituality began being raised as a Catholic. As I look back, I know that my interest in religion was really the beginning of a path. This path would eventually take me from dogma and blind faith to a deep and intimate spirituality that lives within me.

Parents, family, friends, and the geographical location where I was raised did not influence my curiosity about religion, God, Jesus Christ, saints, and martyrs. It all came from within me. Although it was practiced to some extent, Christianity was not followed religiously in my home.

When I was younger, I did undergo some speculation and scrutiny regarding my reasons and motivation for such a gripping interest in religion and God. It was not encouraged in me, and at times, I felt like I was somewhat of a religious fanatic because I felt different.

As I grew older, I did not abandon my closeness to God and religion. This also continued throughout my relationships.

I have always had an inner dialogue and curiosity with spirituality. As a child, throughout adolescence, and now as an adult, I have always felt a hunger for knowledge that was beyond this reality. Subconsciously, at that time, I must have sensed that there was something more than the palpable in front of me.

I know this knowledge has been within me all along. I have access to a universal truth or infinite intelligence. It appears as a gut instinct or tuning into my intuition. It is wisdom, and I rely on this wisdom to guide me through life.

Spirituality is not a desire I possess. It is a deep passion that does not seem to diminish. It can be dormant at times, but however subtle it may be, it is always present. I am always aware

of it. The spirituality that accompanies me through life is strong, and it is synonymous with the desire I possess be in love. I am always seeking the love of my life.

Although spirituality appears religious—and my desires appear worldly and superficial—they are intertwined. One does not exist without the other. Every step of my spiritual evolution is tied to a deep desire to be in love.

Spirituality is examining and unlearning religious beliefs that do not serve your true being.

When you endeavor to question any of your religious beliefs, dogmas, or practices, there is resistance to how these beliefs and practices feel to you. You may begin feeling rigidity in the dogma that has been taught to you, and when you begin feeling this way, a pursuit of the truth ensues. You start asking questions that start to peel away layers of conditioning that did not originate in your true self.

You may research the origins of the religion you were brought up with or study the religious books that relate to that religion. This may help you understand the roots and traditions that formed the written word and the dogmas that accompanied them. You may find that you don't resonate with everything you are discovering. However, instead of entirely rebuking the religion, continue to accept the parts that feel pure in their origin and intent. This can bring a closer and deeper awareness to yourself and your relationship with God.

Along with researching the religion you grew up with, you may also open the search to other religions or different cultures around the world. In doing so, the knowledge and practices you discover can expand your awareness. When this happens, you give your consciousness the opportunity to join in the flow of cosmic consciousness. In the flow of this consciousness, any negative or

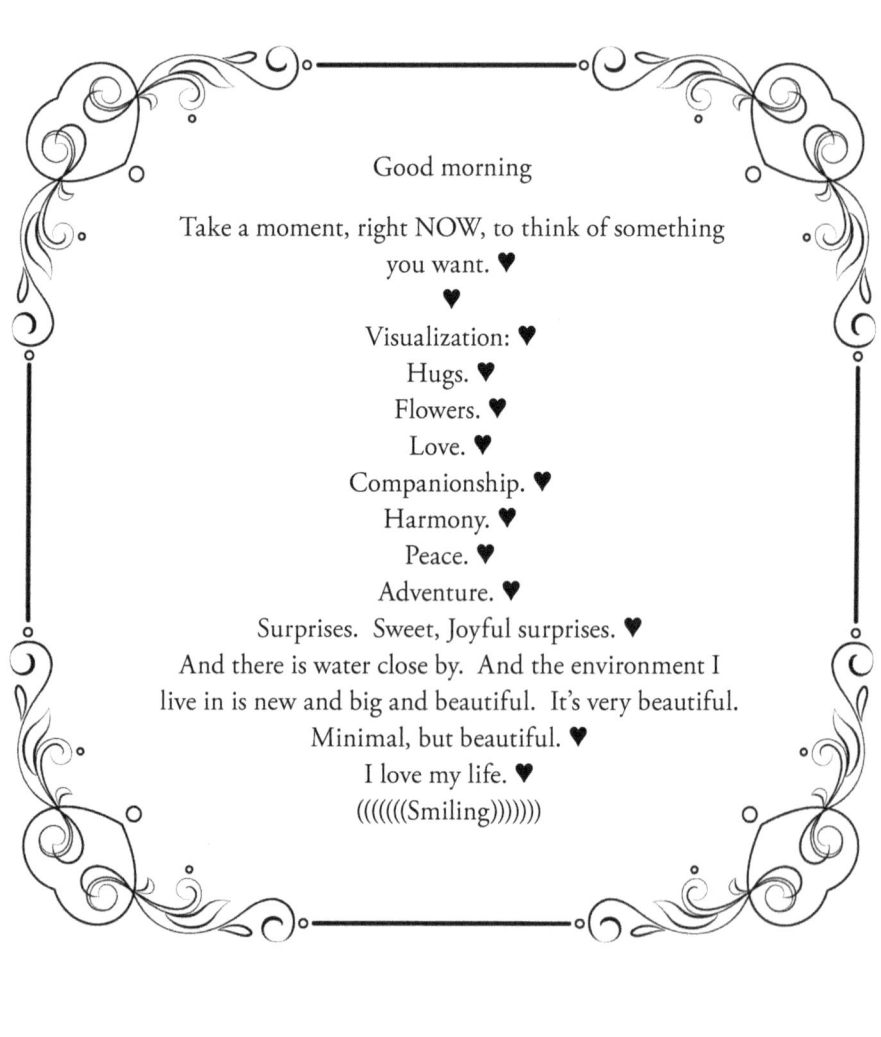

Good morning

Take a moment, right NOW, to think of something
you want. ♥
♥
Visualization: ♥
Hugs. ♥
Flowers. ♥
Love. ♥
Companionship. ♥
Harmony. ♥
Peace. ♥
Adventure. ♥
Surprises. Sweet, Joyful surprises. ♥
And there is water close by. And the environment I
live in is new and big and beautiful. It's very beautiful.
Minimal, but beautiful. ♥
I love my life. ♥
(((((((Smiling)))))))

dark layers of your existence may be cast out—and you can begin getting closer to the light of your being.

As you begin a journey to re-examine your belief systems and unlearn the conditioning you have undergone in your life, you slowly begin uncovering the truth. It is a universal truth. This will grow and evolve until you eventually drop those belief systems altogether and connect to the spring of your internal knowing. This knowing may also be referred to as wisdom, intuition, or infinite intelligence. Your language activates "I know" rather than "I believe." A point of enlightenment is attained where there is an awareness that beliefs are acquired and knowing is eternal.

Spirituality plays an important role in the good-morning messages I send. The process of researching material to create the messages strengthened the components of Christianity that resonated within me. It also expanded my awareness of world religions and cultures. This increased the capability of my mind to learn and hold more universal truths. This allowed more of a knowingness to unravel within me. I carry the wisdom from my true self. I let go of man-made knowledge and connect to the source of all that is.

The spirituality that infuses my good-morning message gives one individual—or maybe all people—the opportunity to tap into the well of universal truth.

Spirituality is connecting with God.

When you decide that you want to live a more spiritual life or live on a more spiritual level, you open the door to a conversation with God. This can lead to one of the most important relationships you participate in your life.

When you begin examining your belief systems and the conditioning surrounding the religion you are born into, it is important to begin to examine your beliefs about God as well.

It is important to begin a practice of conversing with God. This is done through prayer and meditation. Prayer is talking to God, and meditation is listening to God. Through my experience, the most important element in beginning a conversation with God is being honest. You must let go of your perceptions of God.

I began to understand:

- God is not human.
- God does not have feelings or emotions.
- God does not judge.
- God is a being that can listen to me through my mind and heart.
- God is always present within me.

I also understand that being created by God; means you are a piece of God. This 'piece' is your spirit. The intangible element that makes you who you are, I concluded that if you are a piece of God, there is nothing that God does not know about you, and therefore nothing to explain. However, the explanations and conversation are not a way to illuminate God to who you are and what you want, rather, it is an opportunity to put an awareness on knowing your truest self, and the intentions behind your desires. It not only solidifies a relationship with God, but one with your highest self.

Spirituality is the way to return to an authentic relationship with your Creator. When you strengthen your relationship with God, you tap into consciousness that is God. Nothing is more powerful. A relationship with God can be simple and very complex. It is the simplicity of knowing you are loved and protected by God. As you evolve and grow in this relationship, you begin letting go of illusions. Your perceptions of the world, your body, and everything else in between begin to change. As your relationship with God continues to advance, you may begin

Good morning ♥
♥
I trust you God, Universe and myself. ♥
♥
My hearts desires are unfolding, and in this, Iam
happy and fulfilled
Good morning
Stay calm.
I trust that I will be taken care of.

Iam breathing.
Iam alive.
Iam successful.
Iam safe.
Why do I feel this way?
Every day, in every way, Iam in the Universal flow
of all that is good for me and for all.

Blessings on your day and those you love.

embracing the reality that you are everything—and you are nothing. You are in a constant cycle of going from nothingness to complete expansion and back to nothingness.

The good-morning messages are insignificant without my conversations with God. I have embarked on a journey into spirituality that has opened a beautiful relationship with our Creator. I value God, and I am grateful for the awareness that has grown within me and continues to evolve as I move forward in life. I know that I am valued by God and that the whole of creation would be incomplete without me. I trust God. I let go and let him and his wonderful Universe carry me to the core of my truest desires.

With this knowledge and my experiences, it is with my great pleasure that I send my good-morning messages with a piece of God permeated within them to exalt and bless all those who are touched by them.

Spirituality is connecting to my higher self.

When you open yourself to spirituality, it is an opportunity to connect to your true self. It allows you to slowly back up and out of the drama of your life and begin observing yourself in all situations, relationships, and other things around you. You become the witness of your life.

There are a few components that can help you focus within yourself as opposed to seeking approval or validation from outside yourself.

You can self-realize when you observe the quality of your thoughts. Examine them. Question them. Look for the truth. The truth always feels good.

What does it mean when something feels good? It is your instinct. It is an internal tool that allows you to navigate your choices

and the directions you take in your life. It can sometimes be mistaken for *emotional* feeling. A good way to distinguish the two is by understanding that *emotional* feeling are referring to emotions that you, individually, experience. An *intuitive* feeling refers to an intangible, natural response to anything you experience, including people, places, and things—and how they interact with you.

Once you become experienced in distinguishing an emotional feeling to an intuitive feeling, the intuitive feelings are usually positive or negative. They are often referred to as good feelings or bad feelings.

Responding intuitively usually indicates nonrational, insubstantial evidence to measure the response. Most of the time, it doesn't make sense, indicating the source of the feeling is not based on thoughts or provoked by emotions.

An emotional response usually originates from an emotion that translates into a negative or positive thought and can spiral into a whole negative thought process. Here is a simple guide to differentiating between the two:

- Negative *emotional* feeling initiate from thoughts or beliefs that are not true. This includes critical and judgmental thinking.
- Positive *emotional* feeling originate from thoughts and beliefs that are true. This does not include illusory, made-up thoughts and/or beliefs.

Emotional responses can trigger a train of thoughts that increase what may have been a subtle negative (or positive) feeling. As the thought process continues, an eruption of strong emotion occurs, which sometimes cannot be controlled. This is inclusive of overly

Good morning and thank you God ♥

Iam in control of my emotions.
Iam the master of my emotions.

I choose not to let anyone or any situation
influence me or take me away from what I have
to do.

Iam in the Universal flow.
The Universe assists me for my good and the
good of ALL.

excited feelings in positive emotions and exceedingly angry feelings in negative emotions.

The simplicity of observing your thoughts, one by one, is important when you begin the search for self-realization, self-actualization, and enlightenment. This can bring more permanent shifts within you that will result in getting closer and closer to your higher self.

You become more conscious of your instinctual feelings and *emotional* feeling once you can grasp the quality of your thoughts. Your awareness will also expand when you measure the emotions and feelings that result from specific thought processes and beliefs. Repetitive cycles will become evident as you continue practicing self-awareness and mindfulness. These cycles stem from core negative belief systems and conditioning you have acquired through your life. These cycles are directing how you see your reality.

All this observing and witnessing within you is important because it starts a process of detaching layers of negative belief systems and conditioning that shield the true essence of who you are.

It takes time. There are feelings that are difficult to face. There are many tough feelings to get through. However, the reward is great as you transcend these challenges and reach your core, which is pure and exquisite love.

In my experience, spirituality is the key to healing emotional trauma, solving the riddles of your psyche, and strengthening your physical bodies.

I practice spirituality in several ways, including meditation, neurolinguistics programming (self-hypnosis), and analyzing emotional trauma, which is the root cause of any physical ailments I experience.

Of course, I practice spirituality through my good-morning

messages. As I create the message I want to share with the world, I discover and observe more in myself. This allows me to finally break out of my cocoon, revealing a reality that manifests my desires and uncovering who I really am.

Empowerment

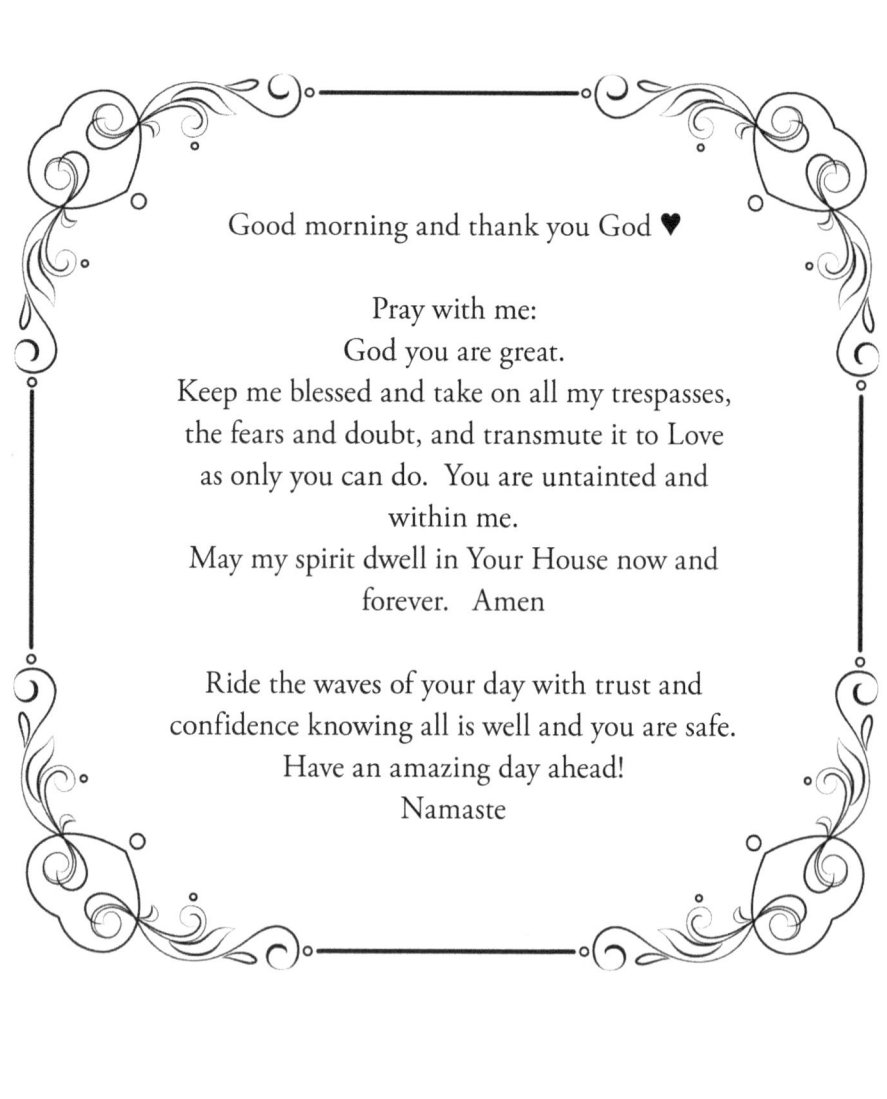

Good morning and thank you God ♥

Pray with me:
God you are great.
Keep me blessed and take on all my trespasses,
the fears and doubt, and transmute it to Love
as only you can do. You are untainted and
within me.
May my spirit dwell in Your House now and
forever. Amen

Ride the waves of your day with trust and
confidence knowing all is well and you are safe.
Have an amazing day ahead!
Namaste

*W*hen I create and share a good-morning message, my intent is empowerment.

Along with a spiritual intent, positivity, and inspiration, I hope you come into an alertness of your own power and that this alertness changes and transforms your life. My wish is that this creates the life you truly deserve.

It took a long time for me to recognize the power that was within me, but I identified this force as the initial component to arising from a sleep state. This triggered the realization of an internal wisdom that I now know is my higher self. As I live from this part of my being, I continue to evolve and manifest more and more of my true desires.

As a child, I was not in touch with this part of myself. My perception of power was instilled by the belief that my mother protected me; therefore, power was outside of me. This train of thought in my *child mind* created the onset of experiences that began my dance with fear. I was afraid of everything when I was not with my mom. As a child, I would describe myself as paralyzed with fear. I was afraid of everything from trying new foods to monsters under my bed, strangers, and even the elderly.

As I grew and continued through elementary school, I eventually became comfortable with my routine and formed some friendships. However, I tended to keep to one person as a close friend and would never label myself a social butterfly. I remember that I did not like any attention being brought to myself. There was an internal fear of criticism of how I looked or anything I said or did. I did love any attention for being smart or special.

As I got older—and toward the end of my elementary school tenure—I felt a strong anger for the injustice and unfairness of the

strong oppressing the weak. This fervent anger was second only to my desire of doing something about it. I wanted to protect and advocate for those who were not able to do so for themselves.

Along with the increased stresses of changing schools and making new friends, my former childhood patterns continued in middle and high school. I kept to one close friend, and I did not like to bring any attention to myself unless it was favorable, which was rare.

I still observed bullying as unjust and unfair, and this has not changed throughout my life, revealing a strong passion to advocate for the weak and those targeted with abuse.

In my younger years, there was little in the way of any real obstacles that required my inner power to be activated. My mother usually handled any sort of conflict in my life. As I got older, I found conflicts difficult to resolve, but I preferred to handle them on my own. I grew more and more resentful of any interference on my behalf.

I felt like I had no voice or control over my life's experiences. An inner conflict began within me during childhood and adolescence, and it triggered guilty feelings. These feelings produced an unconscious use of subtle masks that resulted in a delineation in my relationships and experiences. However, behind the masks, my behavior gradually developed into a tolerance for the sake of conforming and not facing my feelings. There was a façade of harmony, and this created a cyclical pattern that activated a specific reality for me.

As I continued to grow and relate to others, the patterns and behaviors from my early childhood were transferred to most of my developing relationships. I suffered a great deal through my young adulthood and into my forties. Subtle addictions, manipulations, betrayals, heartache, sexual immaturity, and emotional blackmail tainted most—or all—of my experiences. I could not resolve any

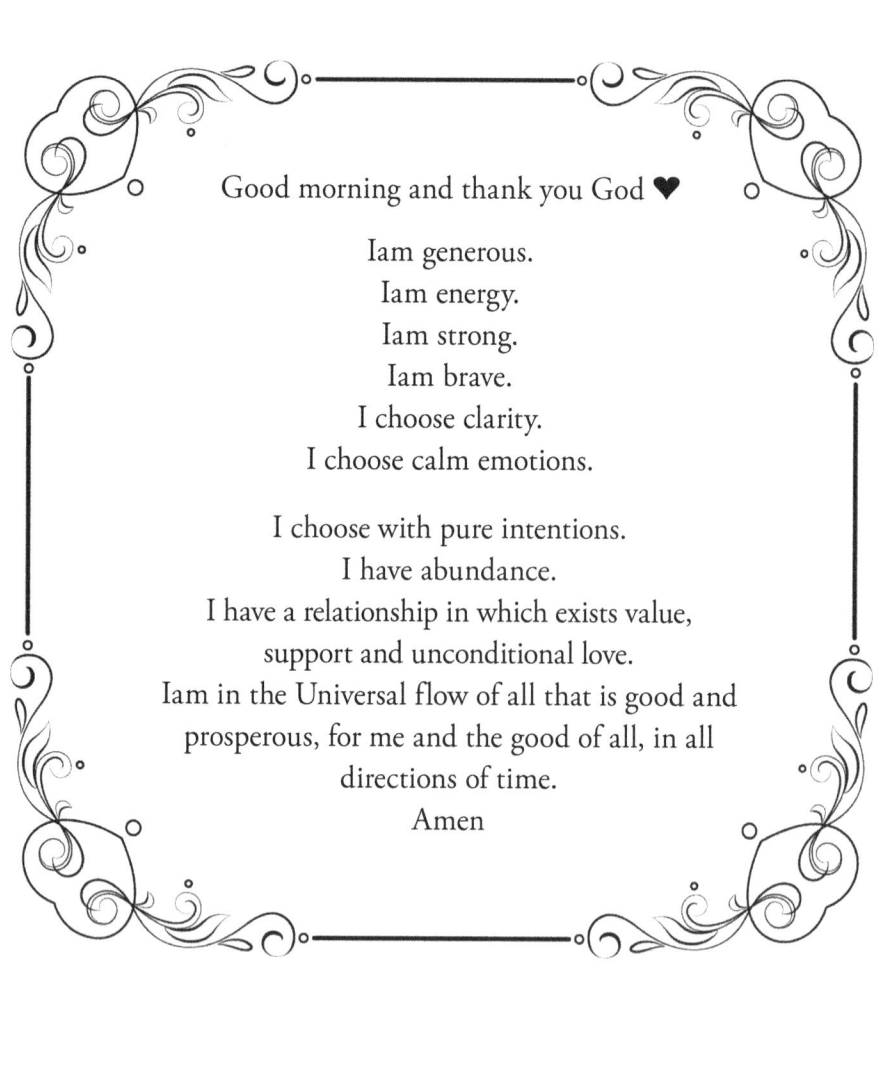

Good morning and thank you God ♥

Iam generous.
Iam energy.
Iam strong.
Iam brave.
I choose clarity.
I choose calm emotions.

I choose with pure intentions.
I have abundance.
I have a relationship in which exists value,
support and unconditional love.
Iam in the Universal flow of all that is good and
prosperous, for me and the good of all, in all
directions of time.
Amen

conflicts in a positive or proactive way, and I did not have the capacity to remove myself from unhealthy relationships. I continuously behaved passively and indifferently to the obvious dysfunction in me and my relationships, the effects were showing up financially and emotionally.

The very last straw was a false belief I created surrounding a decision to change my whole life. I was convinced this would bring me love and happiness. I was rigidly bound to the conviction that this would be the one and only way to live the life I desired. This only ended in more devastation. It was more than I could bear. Terrible decisions, horrible behavior, and defeat spiraled quickly along with an arrogant certainty of a life built in my mind from illusory thoughts and beliefs. It was a fantasy guided by good intentions.

The accumulation of all this loss was detrimental. It almost cost my life. Fortunately, there was a light at the end of the tunnel.

The extreme loss and pain that I felt after this failure was the catalyst that would have me go within to search for the power to lift and eventually rebuild myself. The internal instinct to advocate for the oppressed was always there, but I never realized that I could advocate for and help this weak me. It took many years of counselling, introspection, self-reflection, and contemplation before I recognized what was really going on in my reality.

I allowed people to take control of my life.

I did not advocate for myself in toxic relationships.

I felt like a victim and wanted everyone's sympathy and someone to save me.

I was afraid of being alone and felt that loving a person automatically entitled me to be loved in return.

I did not make anyone accountable for the hurt that was caused to me.

Once I came into this awareness, I took responsibility for my life.

I began deliberately creating what I wanted and who I wanted to be. I do my best to recognize my worth and value by respecting myself. I nurture my soul, which I now know is the source of all my power.

It was paramount that a support system be built to nurture, educate, and cheer me on.

However, ultimately, I had to depend on myself for the support. I understood that if I relied solely on those who were there to do all those things for me, I would just fall back into a pattern of having to find power outside myself. I knew that I would have to be responsible for addressing conflicts, abuse, and toxic relationships from within—and by myself. The support was great, but I had to do it on my own to ensure my own success and a new pattern that was rooted in my own empowerment.

Empowerment is realizing that you are responsible for your own life.

It is imperative to begin looking inward for answers when you are faced with conflict, abuse, or severe instability in relationships or in yourself. It is easy to point fingers and convince yourself that someone else is to blame. You may believe that you are cursed with bad luck or that some higher power (God) is purposely orchestrating your demise. It will surely bring up feelings that lead to thoughts such as no one is listening, you are a victim, you deserve what you are getting (self-loathing), or you subconsciously seek pity and sympathy for the abuse, trauma, and conflict you experienced from others.

However, this is the point where you must take back control of your own life. This means taking responsibility for yourself, becoming accountable for your actions (or nonactions), becoming aware of the choices and decisions you make, and taking responsibility for the consequences that ensue for all your actions and behaviors.

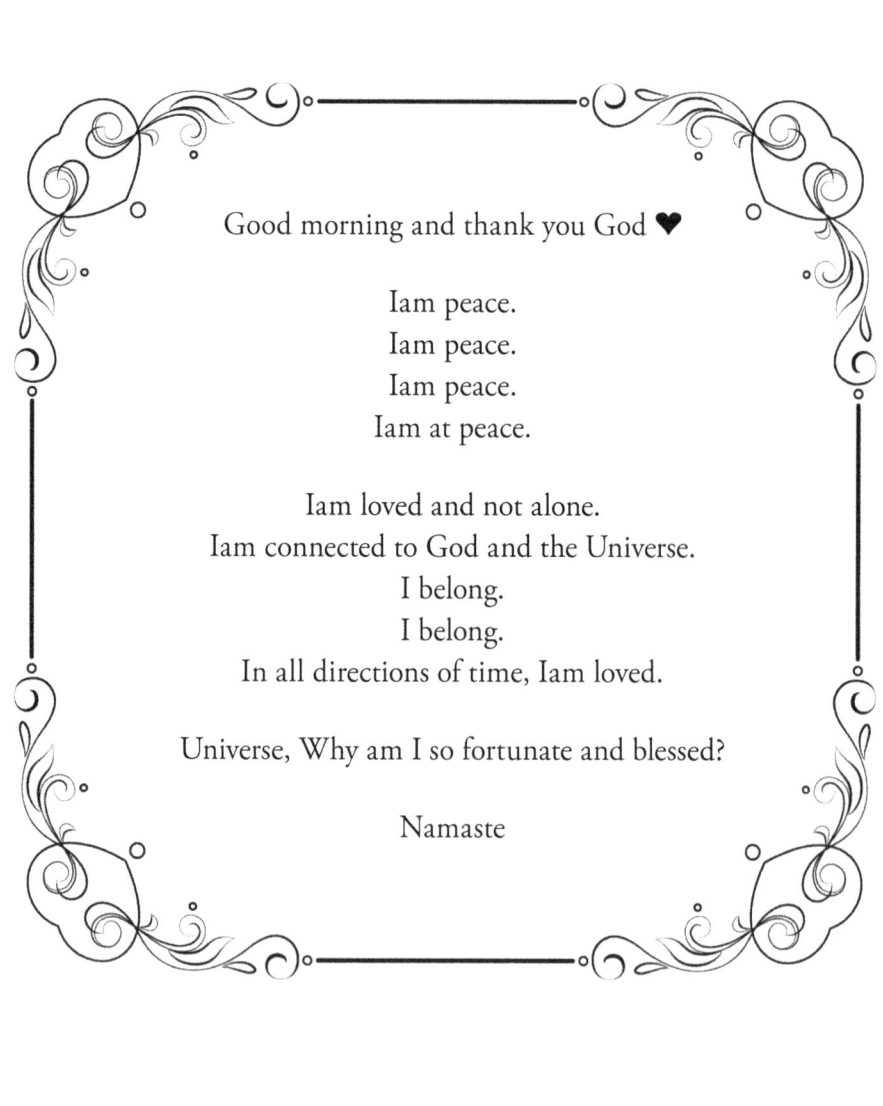

Good morning and thank you God ♥

Iam peace.
Iam peace.
Iam peace.
Iam at peace.

Iam loved and not alone.
Iam connected to God and the Universe.
I belong.
I belong.
In all directions of time, Iam loved.

Universe, Why am I so fortunate and blessed?

Namaste

This is how you empower yourself. It is done by making necessary changes for yourself. It means making a conscious effort to improve your life and to begin deliberately making conscious decisions that create the life you know you deserve.

You begin to understand that you need to take control of yourself instead of enduring an uphill climb through life where only struggle and conflicted relationships are experienced. This replaces a strategy of taking control of others to ensure that you lead a happy, fulfilling life.

You take control of you.

The biggest liberation I ever felt is realizing it is easier to take control of myself than it is to take control of the other 7.5 billion people in the world. This does not invalidate any abuse that may have been inflicted on you or any trauma that you may have experienced.

It is important for a victim of abuse or traumatic experiences to initially receive support, care, and love and to regularly talk about their thoughts and feelings about the experience. It is important that they are given the guidance and knowledge necessary to begin empowering themselves. If a victim is continually pitied and rescued, their own power is being diminished, and that can lead to further similar experiences.

Empowerment comes from within you.

You empower yourself by observing your own thoughts, beliefs, and actions and then beginning to eliminate any thoughts and beliefs that do not serve you. You take an active role in deliberately creating your life. You don't leave anything to chance. You must take responsibility for yourself and your reality and eradicating your belief in victimization. You must believe in your own power.

Empowerment is the ability to look inward. You can validate where and with whom an experience happened, but how you choose to deal with what happened and your feelings and beliefs about it, is completely up to you. No one outside you has the power to choose for you unless you allow them to.

Allowing anyone or anything outside of yourself, the power to choose, fuels their power over you. You don't allow another person to make your choices for you. You don't get in your own way with self-doubt and self-loathing.

Empowerment means eradicating the belief of entitlement. A belief that you are entitled to love comes from feelings of lack and need. Taking responsibility of your life means going within and examining if you seek love from outside yourself and from need. When self love is not present, you will feel a need and desire for it. When this happens, your quest for love becomes a constant pursuit of others and things to fill this void. Because the intentions are lack and need, the effects of the relationships you form will begin showing a pattern of power struggles that stem from fear, conditions, expectations and attachment. You say you have love to give, but it comes with a price to pay. You give, I get. I get, you give. Love is entitled.

Loving yourself is where a feeling of abundance and worth eradicates entitlement. When you can remove the thoughts and beliefs of lack and need, it is not necessary to seek this outside of yourself. In order to give from an intent derived from abundance, you must fill yourself up. You must practice self-respect. You must nurture, care for, and love yourself. Filling yourself up with love and care demonstrates your capability to receive love. This means that you believe that you deserve love.

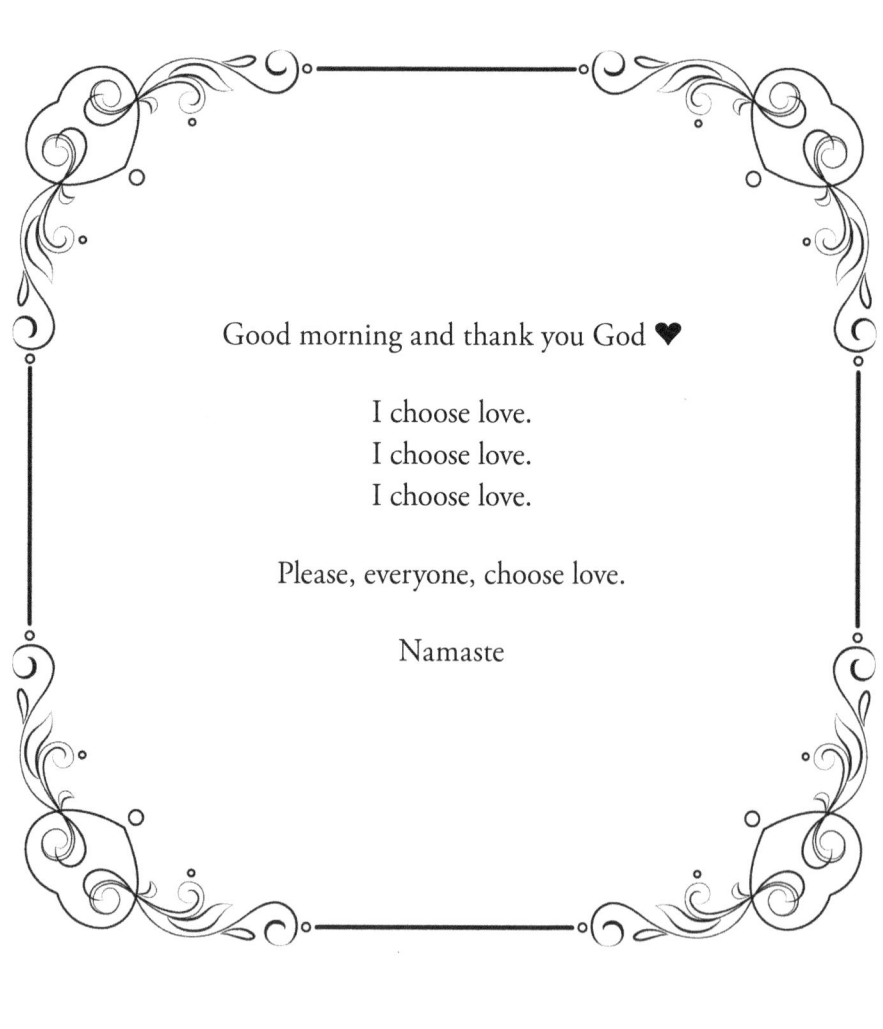

Good morning and thank you God ♥

I choose love.
I choose love.
I choose love.

Please, everyone, choose love.

Namaste

An abundance within yourself creates the intent to unconditionally give.

When you exemplify treating yourself with love, it is an understood guideline for how others are to treat you. Entitlement will transform when you initiate love, respect, and care for yourself. Changes occur that enable an openness to receive as well as give. Knowing that you are worthy of the best—and this is your birthright—helps you evolve and grow with self-love and nurturing.

Empowerment is the ability to live an examined life, which leads to remembering and discovering the truth of your power, which is rooted in an awareness of being eternal.

Empowerment is a multilayered transformation of self. It is the ability to take responsibility for your life, and it is a willingness and desire to examine life and love on a deep level. There are several ways to examine your life. You may be fortunate enough to have been raised with conditioning and beliefs that automatically give you a nonresistant attitude and allow you to reflect, contemplate, and continuously examine your life, the mystery of life, and why it unravels as it does.

At times, examining life and its mysteries is rooted in a dissatisfaction with your life or a rebellion within you that questions your beliefs and conditioning and how you feel they do not serve you.

For some people, it presents as a traumatic event or a relationship that rocks your boat and forces you to look at circumstances or relationships and decide to live your life and enjoy your relationships in a different way.

Whatever the reason, it is a curiosity that is present in the unknowns of the Universe. When you begin examining yourself, your reality, and life itself, you may discover that—along with your

mind and body—a formless and nonphysical part of you that reflects the essence of who you truly are. This usually comes with and aligns with an understanding of a higher power, source energy, or God.

With this awareness of a higher power, source energy, or God, you know there is a part of you that is untainted, pure, and powerful. It is eternal. You develop practices that tap into your own spirit, which is linked with a higher power, source energy, or God. It is an infinite intelligence that is nothing less than divine essence.

You flow with a universal energy that further empowers you to create your life and fulfill a deeper purpose for your existence. The more you can connect on this level, the more your empowerment will grow.

This is true empowerment.

Empowerment is the ability to make a firm decision that validates your worth, value, and respect.

Empowerment is about the choices you make for yourself. When you are faced with a decision, it is important that you know what you want, and it is imperative that you know who you are.

Fortunately, knowing who you are and what you want may have been established early in your life through good guidance, nurturing, love, and care. This will have developed a good sense of self with an early understanding of the spirit within you.

If not, your decisions will reflect a need for what you may have lacked early in your life. It will then be up to you to provide the guidance, nurturing, and love that is required. You must find your spirit, which is often referred to as finding yourself.

Whether early in life or later, feeling worthy, valuable, and respected are key to true self-empowerment.

Good morning and thank you God ♥

Iam confident.
Iam successful.
Iam love.

Iam in the Universal flow.
Iam loved and cherished by God.

In everything I think,
In everything I say,
In everything I do,
Let there be love.

May love wash away all negative and toxic emotions
and feelings right to my core Now.
Iam blessed and may I be a blessing to all I have
met, I meet and have yet to meet.

Namaste

The feeling of worthiness is instilled by an understanding that you are perfect, especially in your imperfections.

Self-worth determines what you deserve in your life and how you are treated.

The feeling of value is instilled by an understanding that you are special and important. It comes from an awareness that you are part of a whole—and the whole is incomplete without you.

Value in yourself determines how you feel about belonging to anyone and the importance of your role in life and the world.

The feeling of respect is instilled by an understanding that you are being heard. It comes from an ability to be aware of how effectively you communicate your worth and value to others.

Self-respect determines how you feel about your body, mind, heart, and time and how they are used by others. Empowering yourself is making firm decisions that are rooted in self-love, being special, and communicating effectively. This will lead to a life that reflects worth, value, and respect.

Empowerment is an important part of the good-morning messages because an important part of empowering yourself is waking up. It is coming into a realization that the subconscious mind must wake up and remain consciously awake. Being consciously awake but remaining in a deep slumber of the subconscious mind will allow mediocrity to creep into you and your reality. It's like moving through life like a robot. You are on automatic pilot and may be buying into an illusion of a world of victimization and self-entitlement. Without this awakening, the empowerment is not sustained.

The power of good-morning messages is all about what I do in the morning when I wake up. It is the power of taking that first moment of awareness and creating my day. It is about reinventing life so that it gives me everything I deserve, and it is my birthright.

It is my choice to create a better me, and ultimately, a better world.

It is my responsibility.

It is my life.

It is my spirit.

That's my power.

The power is in me.

This is true empowerment.

5

Encouragement

Good morning and thank you God ♥

Iam alive.
Iam thoughtful.
Iam mindful.
Iam aware.

It's going to be a great day.
Universe, let's get ready…

*W*hen I send a good-morning message, it provides a message of positivity and empowerment—and it could uplift you with encouragement. When I create the messages and research the material, it's based on how I am feeling. It explains how to respond to a negative emotion or emphasizes a positive emotion I am facing.

By sharing myself and my good-morning messages with the world, I am supporting those who may need to hear words of encouragement. However, the messages are created out of my own need to feel uplifted and supported. It is based on what I need first. When I begin caring for myself first, I remove any attachments and expectations I have from my actions. The intent is pure and true. I realized that sharing my good-morning messages with the world provided me with the support I always wanted and needed.

Encouragement is about emphasizing the positive—and not inflating the negative.

When supporting others, it is important to do so in a way that does not perpetuate the negative emotions they are experiencing. This means not commiserating or engaging in conversations that emphasize negative thoughts about the experiences that triggered the emotions.

Emphasizing the positive reminds these people that they are important to you and all of those who are affected by their lives. You can help them remember their beauty. You want to convey the positive traits they have in order to elevate their spirit and connect them with the good in themselves. You can express to them that they are loved.

It is important to show kindness and concern and offer encouragement that uplifts the spirit. When supporting yourself, it is important to be mindful of your own emotions. When negative emotions arise, it can create and expand an energy that will attract more of those emotions and a reality that matches. They are often suppressed or repressed, and bringing them to the surface is important when you address them.

When you face these emotions, you can begin controlling them. Otherwise, they control you.

Although I am intrinsically happy, I have days when I feel alone, discouraged, exhausted, or drained. I want to be uplifted when I feel that way. Instead of validating negative emotions when I search for images and quotations, I reach for messages that will prompt a positive response. I want to take the focus off negative experiences and bring to light the silver linings. This is key.

Encouragement is a decision to help yourself and put faith in your ability to elevate your feelings and emotions.

There are times in life when you suffer a major loss or heartbreak or experience extreme abuse or toxicity in a relationship that requires support from outside of yourself. The feelings and emotions you may be undergoing are severe, and they weaken your power and ability to see things clearly. It is highly recommended that you find a counselor or therapist who help you cope with your feelings and address them. It is important that they encourage you to help yourself by slowly reconnecting you to your own power and leading you back to your calmness and clarity.

Seeking outside help for traumatic experiences or emotional breakdowns is crucial. This will help provide an environment where you can express your feelings freely and safely. However, the water wings do have to come off.

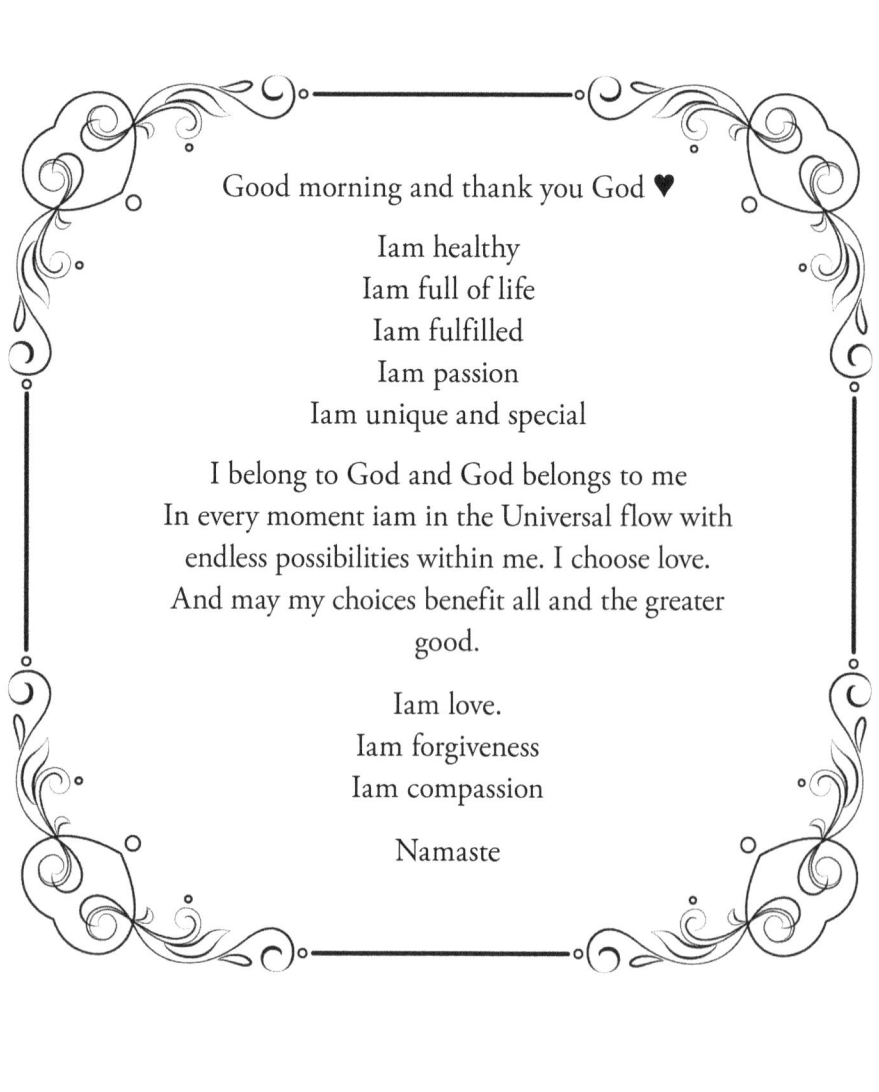

Good morning and thank you God ♥

Iam healthy
Iam full of life
Iam fulfilled
Iam passion
Iam unique and special

I belong to God and God belongs to me
In every moment iam in the Universal flow with
endless possibilities within me. I choose love.
And may my choices benefit all and the greater
good.

Iam love.
Iam forgiveness
Iam compassion

Namaste

Once you move forward from a traumatic event or experience—and time continues to pass—you must develop practices that help you go within to rediscover your own power so that you can help yourself. The feelings and emotions you first felt weaken and diminish as you find the strength to depend on yourself. You avoid victimization and dependency on others and can manage your own life. As you succeed in moving forward, you build faith in your ability to rely on yourself for encouragement and support.

As you move forward and increase your power, you become aware that the power you are harnessing is your spirit. When the source of your power is spirit, it focuses on solutions to problems and uses creativity to address those problems. True power will encourage you to face your fears and your feelings. This provides an illusion-free reality for your life.

I suffered from feelings of hopelessness, and I was an inch away from giving up on life. I did not resist outside help, counseling, and therapy. I experienced a powerful heartbreak that affected my will to live and made me realize that my faith was only an illusion. When the illusion shattered, my heart broke. It felt like it shattered into a million pieces. The heartbreak paralyzed me, but I slowly immersed myself in knowledge and committed to making sure I never had that experience again.

After spending time with my counselor and hypnotherapist, I found it was important to come into my own power. I began seeking practices to deal with my up-and-down mood swings, the highs and lows of my emotions, and with the ebb and flow of my life.

I developed practices that allowed me to put faith in the Universe, in God, and in myself. The more I practiced, the stronger my faith became. I talked to the Universe, and I eventually heard

the Universe answering me. Along with continuing to strengthen my faith, other practices I used were:

- praying to God
- practicing guided meditations that addressed my temporary negative emotions
- reaching out to the world for healing energy
- asking the Universe for support and encouragement

With the good-morning messages, I take my ability to help myself and share it with the world. I want others to see my faith in the Universe and God. I want to share my experiences, take responsibility for my life, and commit to making changes that help create the life God destined me to have.

I am fortunate to have a strong relationship with the Universe. I am grateful and pay forward that gift by sharing it with the world.

Encouragement is being inspired to take a step of courage.

When you are down and depressed, taking a courageous step forward in life and creating a better reality can be monumental. It can be daunting if you are afraid, worried, or suffering from toxic or abusive relationships. The grief and sorrow of loss and heartbreak can be overwhelming.

It is vital that you begin stepping forward after an initial period of processing negative emotions. These experiences are usually catalysts to waking up. It's the fork in the road where you can choose to take control of your life or just live in a default mode. Taking control of your life is about examining any negative thoughts and beliefs. It's choosing to create a better life and better relationships. It is a zealous effort to find inner happiness, peace, and joy. It is finding your inner warrior and facing your fears.

Good morning and thank you God ♥
I choose peace today
I choose harmony today
I choose patience today.
Iam worthy
Iam confident
Iam valuable
Iam a beautiful and wonderful person
Iam seated at the table of life and I belong there.

Living life in a default mode is about stagnating and allowing yourself to be controlled by rigid beliefs, uncontrolled emotions, self-sabotage, and self-doubt. It is letting others take control of you.

As your bravery expands, it will increase your faith in God. You will know that the Universe is instrumental in controlling your life. When you begin believing that there is something bigger than you—the source of all creation and your birthright—you tap into creation for the experience of a happy and peaceful life. You are accessing the power of divine consciousness.

This began for me when I faced the juncture in the path of my life's journey. I knew I had two choices. I knew, deep inside me, that one choice would lead to a downward spiral and end my life. The other choice, no matter how difficult it would be, would move me forward.

As I look back on that decision, it was truly a life-or-death decision. It may not have been a physical death, but my heart would have been broken permanently, which would have been even worse. You cannot live without your heart—physically or emotionally.

I chose then—and I continue to choose—to live. I am so happy I chose to write about my experiences. My journey continues every morning, and I know that my bravery and courage would never have been sustained without my faith, which solidified and increased my ability to tap into divine consciousness.

The power of good-morning messages encouraged me to elevate myself and keep negative emotions from taking control. I learned to reach into myself and tap into my true power—my spirit—and share it with the world.

My good-morning messages give me strength and courage. Every step I have taken—from my heartbreaks to major life decisions and changes—is infused with valor. I continue to walk

into the unknown. I am sometimes afraid, but I never stop moving ahead. When there are moments of disappointment, I just pick up the pieces and keep going. With the desire within me to be with the love of my life, I continue bravely walking forward.

I never give up.

6

K-Creativity

Good morning and thank you God ♥
Iam grateful for another beautiful day of my
life.

*W*ith an intent to close the gap in my search for the love of my life, the good-morning messages came to life. I experienced the joy of creativity, and there was an awakening. I didn't realize my imagination was dormant inside me.

During elementary school, I always looked forward to the weekly art classes we participated in. Coloring, drawing, working with different mediums, and making crafts made me happy. There was always some holiday we focused our attention on so we could create beautiful gifts for our parents and families.

At a young age, I was joyous about creating. I was bursting with even more excitement at the thought of giving it to someone. There was already a sense of pride and fulfillment.

In elementary school, I happily participated in my art classes and would jump at the opportunity to be involved with school pageants and plays. I helped with murals and props, and I sometimes played parts or sang in choirs.

On an individual level, creativity was a positive outlet for me as a child. As I grew older and was able to work collectively with others, the sense of accomplishment and feeling of enrichment grew. I could see our vision coming to life.

As I moved from elementary school into junior high and high school, I did not have the same opportunities to participate and express myself creatively. However, I attempted personal projects such as sketching, sewing, crocheting, knitting, and recording music. I loved creating fashion. I loved the concentration and focus as I was completely immersed in my own world. I was in the zone.

I became less and less interested in pursuing creative projects as I grew into a young adult. Creating things stopped having a place

in my life, and I became completely focused on the personal intimate relationships I was beginning. I was obsessively chasing love.

At that time, I only created by designing and sewing clothes for myself with the help of my mom. I only did this because of my strong desire to continue to be unique and attractive in my new personal relationships. Hair and makeup were the only other unintentional ways I was creative.

As I look back, my ability to be creative was quickly hijacked by my mind. In my new relationships, I was consumed with tormented thoughts, low self-esteem, and insecurities. I was still experiencing the rebellious feelings and emotions from my childhood relationships. I encountered many conflicts at that time in my life.

I felt imprisoned by the control of others. I could never see a way out of situations or relationships I never really wanted. There was no room or time to be creative. I was completely focused on thoughts of being trapped, which did not allow me to see a solution that would work for me in my current emotional state.

There was no awareness of my own power or the power to create my life. It was only recently that I began liberating my old self, creating my own reality, and avoiding being directed by others.

Good intentions and manipulation were the strings through which I was played like a puppet—and the way I behaved with others as well. I know now there were never really any strings there. I always had a choice, but I used my own good intentions and manipulations to fight my feelings of frustration about being trapped. I just didn't know it at the time. My thoughts and beliefs were surrounded by shame, guilt, and an unhealthy definition of loyalty. Feeling trapped was an illusion.

Since that time, I have been working my way back to my true

Good morning and thank you God ♥
Iam blessed.
Iam healthy.
Iam fortunate.

Iam loved and iam loveable.

I love you Universe. I flow with you.
I love you God. I make all my experiences
beautiful for You.

Namaste

and creative self. When I started doing the good-morning messages, I never imagined that I would reconnect with the creativity within me that was quietly waiting to be awakened. The beauty of this awakening was the consciousness that accompanied it. The creativity I experienced as a child expanded and brought great awareness of the limitless possibilities to express imagination and inspiration.

Creativity is an awakening of consciousness.

Creativity can be fulfilling when you endeavor to transform feelings, thoughts, imagination, and inspiration into another form of matter. When you dive into a vision, solution, or invention, you can become completely immersed and separate from your usual thought processes. In a universal flow of consciousness, you are reflective. You move into a mesmerized state. Creativity provides you with an art, and it produces forms of music, dance, and drama. It can provide solutions to problems or challenges and inspire innovation and invention. It is not limited to bringing beauty, solutions, and inventions. It can open you to consciousness through self-awareness.

When you wake up, you become attentive and mindful of yourself. This means taking responsibility for what you create, which can change the intent behind what you are doing. Self-awareness also gives you an opportunity to jump right into the flow of divine consciousness, access infinite intelligence, and connect with the power of the divine and all its universal truths. This can change the impact and benefit of all that is created.

Whatever you set out to create, you can add the element of mindfulness. Your consciousness will expand and evolve. When you know that you are accessing infinite intelligence for imagination and inspiration, success is eventual.

Once you wake up, you can access divine consciousness with ease. As your mindfulness continues to grow, you bridge and close the gap to your true self. When you create from a place of self-awareness and consciousness, you open yourself to a true connection with the source of creativity: God. You continually get closer to God, and the purpose that you are set out to fulfill becomes more apparent.

When I began creating the good-morning messages, my awareness began growing and evolving. At first, I didn't realize it because I had been immersed in the same process as a child and adolescent. As I continued to be creative, practice meditation, and explore my spiritual journey, I felt more and more inspired. I experienced a visible synchronicity with the Universe. The value of self-awareness became clearer, which led to an expanded consciousness. I was experiencing a flow of alert creativity, which enabled the messages to have a pure intent with universal truths that blended inherently in every word and image.

Creativity is an expression of your true self.

Creativity is a tool that can help you express who you truly are. You can deliberately create the life you were destined to lead.

When you endeavor to express yourself creatively, you are giving yourself an opportunity to tap into your true self. When creativity is initiated, it can come from the many layers that have made you who you are. It can come from thoughts, beliefs, and conditioning you have acquired in life. It can come from your emotions: happy, joyous, and peaceful or sad, angry, and anxious.

Creativity can be required for learning, finding answers to problems, and discovering ingenuity. You can also create yourself and your reality. This type of creating forces you to dive into parts of yourself that are untouched, unfelt, or unknown. It is removing all the thoughts, beliefs, and emotions you have accumulated in

Good morning and thank you God ♥
I choose rest today.
I choose joy today.
I choose beauty today.
IAM faithful.
IAM devoted.
If the love of my life is God, then all of Gods
creation are the love of my life.
IAM fortunate.

Namaste

life. They have covered your true self. Your true self is part of God. It is untainted, pure, and eternal. It is full of power and the wisdom of universal truths. When you start creating from the pieces of your spirit, you expose the truth of who and what you really are.

The first messages I created were intended to attract a good morning from the love of my life. I never imagined that expressing myself creatively through these messages would grow and evolve into a process that would serve me by affirming who I really am. The more I follow this creative path, the more I discover a journey that allows me to design a fulfilling life that embodies love and purpose.

Creativity is a connection with divine consciousness.

Divine consciousness is what you access as you begin any creative purpose. Divine consciousness can refer to cosmic consciousness, infinite intelligence or emotional intelligence. It is the flow of the Universe. Just as God resides within you as an expression of who you are, so does divine consciousness. It is a part of you and is always available to you.

Creativity emerges from your thoughts, beliefs, and emotions, and it is the spring of divinity from which inspiration and imagination are born. When you open yourself to self-awareness and your own consciousness, you open limitless possibilities to infuse your creativity. Divine consciousness is a connection you make with God. By doing this, you permeate anything you create with a piece of God and the universal truths that accompany God.

When I followed my burning desire to be with the love of my life, I unknowingly accessed divinity within me. I had no idea how these good-morning messages would affect me. As I continued to produce the messages, I grew spiritually. My spiritual journey continued to elevate me from an egotistical girl to a self-aware soul.

There is so much more to elevate in myself and my reality, but as I become the witness of my life and the observer of my world, there is no turning back. As I imbued self-awareness and mindfulness and connected to the divine, this sleeping beauty awakened.

Moving forward, as I have always done, I am inspired as a warrior princess of God to awaken as many souls as possible. I don't know how it will all happen, but I know—without a doubt—that God is accompanying me.

7

Evolution

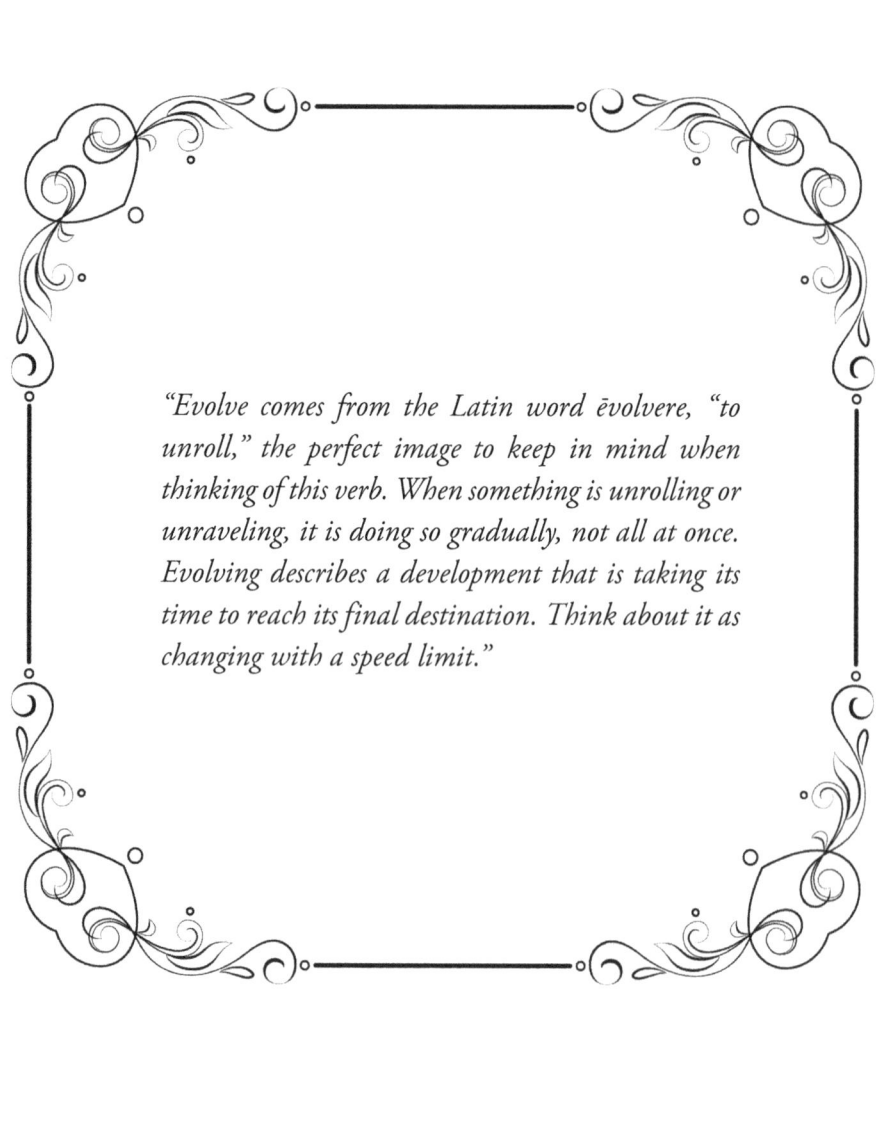

"Evolve comes from the Latin word ēvolvere, "to unroll," the perfect image to keep in mind when thinking of this verb. When something is unrolling or unraveling, it is doing so gradually, not all at once. Evolving describes a development that is taking its time to reach its final destination. Think about it as changing with a speed limit."

*E*volution. What exactly does this mean? The evolution of the soul is backward, and in my experience, I have discovered that it all begins with an awakening. We are born into life and the world, but our consciousness is asleep. The body and mind appear to function consciously, but there is no awareness of the true being within.

So, I am awake now. I am self-aware now. And the season of evolution approaches. I am unrolling. I am gradually unraveling myself. My evolution moves slowly and steadily, and the destination is not a new and better place; rather, it is the place where I originated. It is my true being.

In unraveling myself, I discover the blueprint of creating and designing my life. The details illustrate a clear purpose and provide the means to propel me forward.

This season will come with joyful and positive new thoughts and beliefs and an unwavering faith in all the possibilities of the Universe and what it orchestrates on my behalf through my choices, behaviors, and attitudes.

There will be no tolerating life. There will be reverence for life and all its beauty.

There will be no suffering. It will be a time of enjoyment and playfulness with the Universe, God, life, the beauty of eventually creating from the light of my true being, and fulfilling desires that are divinely ordained.

Does this lead to the love of my life?

Maybe.

There is hope and trust that all is well in my world—now and always.

a.a.

About the Reading List

The authors of said books have been true mentors, and are instrumental in catapulting my life to the Divine truths that are buried deep within me.

They literally, reached in and WOKE ME UP.

THANK YOU for sharing the wisdom of the Universe.

The meditations may not work for everyone. I selected the ones that are most powerful to break down negative core beliefs on a subconscious level.

Caution is exercised when attempting any work on the subconscious through any medium. If you are not ready, it's best to wait until you are.

And hypnosis is no substitute for seeking medical attention.

a.a.

Reading List and Online Meditations

Byrne, Rhonda. The Secret : The 10th Anniversary Edition. New York, Ny, Atria Books ; Hillsboro, Or, 2016.

Chopra Center. "Oprah & Deepak's 21-Day Meditation Experience, Desire and Destiny." YouTube, 11 Nov. 2013, www.youtube.com/watch?v=jUCu-9MG1Lc.

Deva Premal & Miten. "Deva Premal & Miten - 21-Day Mantra Meditation Journey - How Mantras Work." YouTube, 10 Sept. 2013, www.youtube.com/watch?v=P-tn4KQeVbI.

Dooley, Mike. More Notes from the Universe : Life, Dreams, and Happiness. Hillsboro, Or., Beyond Words Pub, 2008.

Gilbert, Elizabeth. Eat, Pray, Love : One Woman's Search for Everything across Italy, India and Indonesia. New York, Riverhead Books, 2017.

Hay, Louise L. Heal Your Body : The Mental Causes for Physical Illness and the Metaphysical Way to Overcome Them. Carlsbad, Calif., Hay House, 2012.

---. Wisdom Cards : A 64-Card Deck. Carlsbad, Ca, Hay House, Inc, 2000.

a.a.

Hicks, Esther, and Jerry Hicks. The Astonishing Power of Emotions : Let Your Feelings Be Your Guide. Carlsbad, Calif., Hay House, 2008.

Hill, Napoleon. Think and Grow Rich by Napoleon Hill. New York: Fawcett Books (Mm, 1990.

Meditative Mind. "3 Powerful Healing Mantras - Physical Emotional and Spiritual Healing | Meditative Mind." YouTube, 15 Dec. 2015, www.youtube.com/watch?v=Cvoa6PWiKWg.

Neale Donald Walsch. The Complete Conversations with God : An Uncommon Dialogue. Charlottesville, Va, Hampton Roads Pub. Co. ; New York, 2005.

Sealey, Michael. "Hypnosis for Clearing Subconscious Negativity." YouTube, 24 Sept. 2014, www.youtube.com/watch?v=FiPDV9L5qpQ.

"TINA Turner Blog." YouTube, 2019, www.youtube.com/user/TinaTurnerBlog

Tolle, Eckhart. The Power of NOW : A Guide to Spiritual Enlightenment. Vancouver, B.C., Namaste Pub. ; Novato, Calif, 2004.

a.a.

THE SEVEN CELESTIAL SPHERES